YOUNG PROFILES

LeAnn Rimes

Tamara L. Britton
ABDO Publishing Company

visit us at
www.abdopub.com

Published by ABDO Publishing Company 4940 Viking Drive, Edina, Minnesota 55435.
Copyright © 1999 by Abdo Consulting Group, Inc. International copyrights reserved in
all countries. No part of this book may be reproduced in any form without written
permission from the publisher.

Printed in the United States.

Photo credits: AP/Wide World; Shooting Star

Edited by Paul Joseph
Contributing editor A.T. McKenna

Library of Congress Cataloging-in-Publication Data

Britton, Tamara L., 1963
    LeAnn Rimes / Tamara L. Britton.
    p. cm. -- (Young profiles)
    Includes index.
    Summary: A biography of the young country music star who was the youngest
artist and only country performer ever to win the Grammy Award for Best New
Artist.
    ISBN 1-57765-325-4 (hardcover)
    ISBN 1-57765-337-8 (paperback)
    1. Rimes, LeAnn--Juvenile literature. 2. Country musicians--United States--
Biography--Juvenile literature. [1. Rimes, LeAnn. 2. Musicians. 3. Women--
Biography. 4. Country music.] I. Title II. Series
    ML3930.R56B75   1998
    782.421642'092--dc21
    [B]   98-40385
                                  CIP
                                  AC MN

Contents

A Teenage Sensation

In 1996, LeAnn Rimes burst onto the charts with her smash hit album *Blue*. Her beautiful voice and her mature **demeanor** made her seem much older than she was. But LeAnn was only 14 years old!

This multi-talented superstar went from a talented five year-old to a Grammy Award winning performer in just 10 years. Her quick rise to fame has been carefully managed by her loving parents.

How did this polite young woman go from small-town Mississippi girl to the reigning queen of country music? LeAnn's drive, determination, and desire to be a star, along with the help of her close-knit family, **propelled** her to the top. It all began in a Mississippi town called Jackson.

*LeAnn Rimes at Radio City Music Hall for
the 40th annual Grammy Awards.*

Young Profile:
LeAnn Rimes

Name: LeAnn Rimes

Parents: Wilbur and Belinda Rimes

Birth Date: August 28, 1982

Place of Birth: Jackson, Mississippi

Hair: Blond

Eyes: Blue

Height: 5 feet 5 inches

Hobbies: Horseback riding, softball, shopping, going to concerts

Opposite page: LeAnn Rimes
is one of the hottest singers in
country music.

LeAnn's Family

LeAnn's father's name is Wilbur and her mother's name is Belinda. Wilbur and Belinda were sweethearts in high school. After high school they decided to get married.

Wilbur worked for an oil company and Belinda worked as a receptionist. They wanted to start a family right away. They had to wait longer than they wanted to, but finally Wilbur and Belinda were blessed with a beautiful daughter. LeAnn was born on August 28, 1982 in Jackson, Mississippi.

Both of LeAnn's parents had an interest in music. Belinda liked to sing and Wilbur played the guitar. With her mother singing to her and her father singing and playing guitar, it wasn't long before LeAnn's talent began to show. At the age of only 18 months, she began singing "Jesus Loves Me" along with her mom!

LeAnn was born in Jackson, Mississippi.

A Natural from Jackson

LeAnn's singing only got better. LeAnn's father recorded her singing when she was young. LeAnn said later, "I could sing better than I could talk." At the age of five, LeAnn's interest in music was increasing. She entered a song and dance contest.

LeAnn sang the song "Getting to Know You" at the contest. She won the first place trophy for her **performance**! At only four feet (1.2 m) tall, LeAnn had a hard time carrying the six foot (1.8 m) tall trophy into her house.

LeAnn's success in the contest convinced her that she wanted to go into show business. She wanted to become a star. In order to give LeAnn the best chance at success, her family decided to move to Texas.

LeAnn Rimes in concert.

Off to Texas

When LeAnn was six, her family moved to Garland, Texas. Garland is a town near Dallas. While in Texas, LeAnn focused not only on singing, but also on acting. She **auditioned** for the musical *Annie II* in New York, and played the character Tiny Tim in a production of Charles Dickens's *A Christmas Carol* in Dallas.

When LeAnn was eight years old, she was able to combine her singing and acting talents on the television show *Star Search*. The producers of the show found the star they were searching for when LeAnn won the competition two weeks in a row singing the song "Don't Worry About Me."

LeAnn continued to display her amazing talents by performing in the *Johnnie High Country Musical Review*. She also sang the "Star Spangled Banner" *a cappella* at events around town. She sang at Dallas Cowboys football games, the Walt Garrison Rodeo, and at the National Cutting Horse

Championships. LeAnn was amazingly talented, and soon her father decided she was ready to record an album.

LeAnn Rimes was not only a talented singer but also did some acting as a young child.

The First Album

LeAnn's father produced her first album. He chose to work in a studio in Clovis, New Mexico. Lyle Walker ran the studio. Lyle and Wilbur agreed to manage LeAnn together.

A local disc jockey named Bill Mack had heard LeAnn sing at a Dallas Cowboys game. Bill had written a song called "Blue" in the 1960s for a country singer named Patsy Cline. But Patsy died in a plane crash before she could record Bill's song. He offered it to LeAnn to sing. She recorded the song on her album.

LeAnn's first album, called *After All*, was released in 1994. It was successful in the **marketplace** around Texas. LeAnn's dad drove her around Texas in an old bus to sing the songs from *After All* at concert appearances. The album impressed many people, and LeAnn signed a contract with MCG/Curb records.

LeAnn Rimes started her career singing in Texas.

Blue

LeAnn's first album for her new label included two songs from *After All*, "Blue" and "I'll Get Even With You." She also sang a song she cowrote with Ron Grimes and Jon Rutherford called "Talk To Me." Another highlight of the album was a duet with country music legend Eddy Arnold, singing his song "Cattle Call." "Eddy Arnold was great," LeAnn said later. "He kind of adopted me as his granddaughter and then as his daughter."

The first single released from the album was the song "Blue," and it raced into the top 10 on the singles charts. The album, also called *Blue*, was released on July 9, 1996, and **debuted** at number three on the *Billboard 200*.

The success of the album *Blue* got the attention of many country artists. LeAnn was in demand to appear in concerts with top performers.

LeAnn Rimes accepts her Horizon Award at the Country Music Association Awards Show in Nashville in 1997.

The Awards

In 1996, the Country Music Association Awards **nominated** LeAnn's song "Blue" for single of the year. She was also a finalist for the Horizon Award. While she did not win either award, her **performance** on the awards show made many people notice her talent. And the **recognition** was soon to follow.

In 1997, LeAnn was awarded the Grammy Award for Best New Artist of 1996. She was both the youngest artist and the only country performer ever to win this award. She also took home the award for Best Female Country Vocal Performance for the song "Blue."

LeAnn shined at the American Country Music Awards. She won Best New Female Vocalist, and Single of the Year and Song of the Year awards for "Blue." At the American Music Awards, LeAnn was named Best Country Newcomer. At the Country Music Association Awards, she won the Horizon Award. The talented singer from Mississippi was finally a star.

LeAnn Rimes holds her Best New Artist and Best Female Country Vocal Performance awards during the 39th Annual Grammy Awards in New York in 1997.

More Albums

LeAnn continues to enjoy success with her music. With her hits "Blue," "You Light Up my Life," and "Unchained Melody," she became the first country artist to have three consecutive number one **debuts** on the country charts.

You Light Up My Life—Inspirational Songs debuted at number one on the country, pop, and Christian charts. This is the first time ever an album has debuted in the top spot on all three charts.

LeAnn continues to expand her boundaries as a musician. Her fourth album, *Sittin' on Top of the World*, includes a cover of "Purple Rain." This song was made famous by the Artist Formerly Known as Prince in the movie *Purple Rain*.

Opposite page: LeAnn Rimes has crossed over from country to pop music.

Smashing Success

LeAnn's fans flock to record stores to buy the latest release by their favorite singer.   About 125,000 LeAnn Rimes albums are sold each week!

Blue is quadruple platinum. An album is termed platinum when one million copies are sold. *Blue* has sold nearly five million copies!

Two of LeAnn's other albums are multi-platinum, too. Her second album, *Unchained Melody,* has sold more than two million copies. *You Light Up My Life—Inspirational Songs* has also sold over two million copies. Her latest release *Sittin' on Top of the World* is already platinum, and is heading toward the multi-platinum mark of two million copies sold.

LeAnn Rimes, center, poses for pictures with fans at her autograph booth at the International Country Music Fan Fair Festival in Nashville, Tennessee.

A New Life

LeAnn's incredible success has changed her life. After the release of *Sittin' on Top of the World*, she began a 100 city tour. With her huge success, she has traded the old bus she used to travel in for a huge new bus. It has a kitchen, a bedroom, a shower, and a washer and dryer!

Besides music, LeAnn continues to **pursue** her dream of acting. She wrote a Christmas story called *Holiday in Your Heart*. The tale was made into a TV movie in 1997, and LeAnn was the star.

She has also acted in several episodes of the daytime **serial** *Days of Our Lives*. She turned down a role in the movie *The Horse Whisperer* because her parents thought she already had enough to do.

LeAnn has to budget her time since the successful turn her singing career has taken. Her life is now very busy. But with her musical talent and drive, LeAnn will be a force in the music industry for a long time to come.

LeAnn at the 1997 Country Music Awards.

Future Plans

LeAnn has gone from a singing toddler to an international star. She has sold more than nine million albums. She already has two Grammy Awards. What could be next for her?

As busy as she is, LeAnn is making plans for the future. "I want to continue singing and writing songs," she says. She also wants to continue acting.

LeAnn is not overlooking the importance of an education. She considers college a possibility. She is interested in working with children and says "I have thought about studying speech pathology." Whatever road LeAnn chooses in the future, she is sure to be a huge success.

Opposite page: LeAnn Rimes performs "How Do I Live" at the 40th Annual Grammy Awards at New York's Radio City Music Hall, 1998.

Fun Facts

• LeAnn's real name is Margaret. LeAnn is her middle name.

• LeAnn has a dog named Sandy.

• LeAnn's favorite dessert is a strawberry ice cream soda.

• In Australia, LeAnn is the highest selling female act in country music history!

LeAnn heads for first during the City of Hope celebrity softball game in Nashville.

Opposite page: LeAnn enjoys a strawberry ice cream soda.

Glossary

A cappella: an Italian word that means singing without instrumental accompaniment.

Auditioned: a short performance to show ability in order to get a part in a movie, a play, or a band.

Debut: the first appearance.

Demeanor: the way a person behaves.

Marketplace: an area of the business world where people buy things.

Nominated: to be proposed as a possible winner of an award.

Performance: a presentation before an audience.

Propelled: something that is moved forward.

Pursue: to strive to obtain or accomplish something.

Recognition: attention or favorable notice.

Serial: a drama shown in installments at regular intervals.

Internet Sites

www.rimestimes.com
This is a must see website for all LeAnn Rimes fans. This fantastic official website will take weeks to get through plus it is always being updated. Listen to her hit songs, get on her mailing list, join her fan club, checkout her concert dates and see when she is coming to your town. This can all be done right at your home on your computer!

www.geocities.com/Hollywood/Hills/6178/
Great photos, wonderful biography, concert dates, and a lively chat room are all on this excellent webpage dedicated to country's hottest star—LeAnn Rimes.

www.geocities.com/CollegePark/Union/4364/leannrimes.html
Checkout this fun website dedicated to LeAnn Rimes. Get all of the facts about the young queen of country, plus tour dates, pictures, newsletters, even the lyrics to LeAnn's songs.

These sites are subject to change.

Pass It On

Tell readers around the country information you've learned about your favorite superstars. Share your little-known facts and interesting stories.
We want to hear from you!
To get posted on the ABDO Publishing Company website E-mail us at
"Adventure@abdopub.com"
Download a free screen saver at www.abdopub.com

Index